Girls and their Horses

★ American Girl®

Published by Pleasant Company Publications

Copyright © 2000 by American Girl, LLC

Questions or comments? Call 1-800-845-0005,
visit **americangirl.com**, or write to
Customer Service, American Girl,
8400 Fairway Place, Middleton, WI 53562-0497.

Printed in China
08 09 10 11 12 LEO 11 10 9 8 7 6

All American Girl marks are trademarks
of American Girl, LLC.

Editorial Development: Camela Decaire, Michelle Watkins

Art Direction and Design: Mengwan Lin

Book Production: Lori Armstrong, Paula Moon

Illustrations: David Austin Clar

Photography: Cover and title page, © 2000, James Leslie
Parker; p. 4, Richard Nugent; Rodeo Riders (pp. 6–15),
James Cammack; Wild Ponies (pp. 16–25), Medford Taylor;
p.17, book cover photo by Jamie Young; Mini Horses (pp.
26–33), David Schreiber; Vaulters (pp. 34–41), Eric Jewett;
p. 36, Clydesdale, © Gemma Giannini, from Grant Heilman
Photography, Inc.; Show Jumper: p. 42, © 2000 James Leslie
Parker; p. 44, over poles, © Dorling Kindersley; pp. 46–49,
© O'Neill's; p. 50, Reflections of Killington; Horse Chores
(pp. 52–61), Richard Nugent; Horse Sense: Appaloosa,
Palomino, Bay, Chestnut, Black, Blue Roan, Gray, and Gray
showing points, © Gemma Giannini, from Grant Heilman
Photography, Inc.; Strawberry Roan, © Larry Lefever, from
Grant Heilman Photography, Inc.; White, Dun, and Brown,
© 1998 by Marty Felix.

Stories in this book have been previously published in
American Girl magazine.

You love horses. You dream of caring for a horse, spending hours in a **barn** and in the **saddle**. You know you and your horse would make a perfect **team.** But there's a lot more to owning and riding a horse than you might think. It takes time and **training** and **dedication** to become a good rider and a good friend to a horse. In this book you'll meet real girls—and their horses—who know about all the hard work! But they also know the work pays off. Discover the rewards for yourself as you read these true stories, collected from the pages of *American Girl* magazine. From rodeos to jumping shows, these perfect teams are making their dreams come **true.**

Dear Reader

Contents

Rodeo Riders

Welcome to the Little Britches Rodeo finals. Nine-year-old Lindsay C. and her sister Jennifer have worked all summer to be here. Now the Colorado sun is glaring, the crowd is roaring, and it's time to ride. As her name is called, Lindsay and her horse, Coyote, leap forward, weaving together through a racecourse of six tall poles, trying to get to the finish line as gracefully and swiftly as they can.

High Stakes

The Little Britches Rodeo is the biggest kids' rodeo in America. Getting here is a big achievement. Lindsay spends each summer traveling with her mom and sister to more than 30 local rodeos. There she and her sister compete against other kids in six different events. If they place first or second in an event, they earn the right to compete at finals at the end of the season. The stakes are high at finals—every rider is dreaming of winning prizes like saddles and college scholarships.

The Six Big Events

Pole Bending

Girls must ride their horses through a course of six poles set up 21 feet apart, weaving in and out. If a rider bumps into a pole, she can grab it and keep it from falling, but if it actually falls down, she's charged a five-second penalty.

Barrel Racing

Riders must guide their horses around three barrels in a cloverleaf pattern, handling sharp turns at top speed.

Trail Course

As she rides a set trail, a girl must open and close a gate, put mail into a mailbox, back her horse between two barrels, run over a bridge, and get home—all in about 24 seconds.

Goat Tying

As fast as she can, a rider races toward a goat tied to a post in the middle of the arena. She jumps off her horse while it's still moving, throws the goat to the ground, and ties three of its legs together. Don't worry, the goat doesn't get hurt!

Ranch Skills

Rodeo events are based on skills ranchers use every day. But even the most experienced hand never knows quite what to expect. A calf might refuse to run, a goat might be unbeatably stubborn, a horse might not get up to speed. It's all part of the fun.

Dally Ribbon Roping

Girls partner up for this event. A "roper" lassos a calf with her right hand and does a "dally," or wraps the extra rope around her saddle horn. A "runner" races over to the calf, grabs a ribbon that's tied to its tail, and runs back to her starting box.

Breakaway Calf Roping

A girl ties one end of a rope to her saddle horn. She uses the rest of the rope to lasso a running calf by the neck. When she's got the calf, she quickly brings her horse to a stop so the rope will "break away" from her saddle horn. Timing stops when the rope hits the ground.

Rodeo Gear

Lindsay is well prepared for her events. Leather boots with high heels keep her feet from slipping through her saddle's stirrups as her horse turns and sprints, and a wide-brimmed hat shields her eyes from the sun.

She uses a Western saddle, which has a deep seat and long stirrups so that it is comfortable to sit on. It was originally designed for cowboys, who had to spend days in the saddle rounding up cattle. The wide skirt spreads the rider's weight across the horse's back, so the horse can bear the weight for long distances.

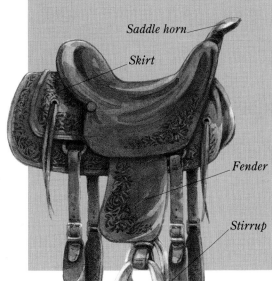

Saddle horn

Skirt

Fender

Stirrup

The Challenge

No amount of preparation can guarantee all will go well in competition though, as Lindsay well knows. For her, barrel racing is always tough. She rides a different horse, Colorado, for barrel racing. Colorado is blind in one eye, so he counts on Lindsay's skill to lead them into first place. Lindsay has to help him figure out when to turn around the barrels.

Too Fast

Lindsay and Colorado make it through the course once. But when it's time for their second race, something goes wrong. Concentrating, Lindsay tries to keep up with Colorado's speed, guiding him carefully. But it is too much too fast. Lindsay forgets a signal, and Colorado turns too soon. They miss a barrel and their disappointment is obvious.

Winners

It's a tough break, but Lindsay gets over it. There's too much else going on. Now she's happy to root for her sister. Jennifer has a few problems in the goat-tying event, but by the end of the week she's World Champion Pole Bender and World Champion All-Around Cowgirl!

The End

In some ways the Little Britches finals are like one big party. After the summer of competing, Lindsay knows almost everyone there. But she's ready for the end, too. Rodeos are exciting, but exhausting! On the last day, the sisters load up their horses and say good-bye to all their friends. Then, like true cowgirls, they ride off into the sunset—until the next rodeo.

Mandy A. is seeing fiction come to life. Standing on the shore of tiny Chincoteague Island, she's seeing her very own Misty of Chincoteague swim ashore. *Misty of Chincoteague*, a book by Marguerite Henry, tells the story of two children and some very special wild ponies.

A Pony Tale

Misty of Chincoteague has captured the imagination of millions of people for more than 50 years, and now, every summer, tourists flock to tiny Chincoteague Island, Virginia, during the last week of July to see the story come true. Mandy is part of the crowd, but she's not just here to watch. She's come to Chincoteague to take home a pony!

Mystery

No one's sure how the ponies first got to Assateague Island. One legend says they swam ashore from a Spanish shipwreck. Others say the ponies are descendants of horses turned loose by early settlers. After the auction, the horses get back to Assateague by swimming again. There they'll live free for another year—until the next roundup.

Assateague Island

The ponies live on Assateague Island, a quarter mile away from Chincoteague. Assateague is a wildlife refuge where the ponies live free year-round. "Cowboys" (really firefighters from Chincoteague) care for them. They feed them in harsh weather and pay for veterinary care. Every July, they sell some of the ponies at an auction to raise money. The auction also helps to keep the ponies from overpopulating the island. This year the cowboys have rounded up about 150 horses to sell.

The Roundup

Mandy's already picked out the pony she'd really like to have. While she's realistic—she has six backup choices!—a golden foal with a creamy white mane and tail has already captured her heart. But this morning, she can't even spot her. It's early in the morning when the ponies suddenly come pounding down Assateague Island's shore.

The Swim

The horses plunge into the water, neighing and whinnying, for the quarter-mile swim to Chincoteague. It's an amazing sight. In just six minutes the first horses reach the shore. "They look so different when they're wet!" says Mandy.

The Auction

After a rest, the ponies are herded to the Chincoteague fairground for the auction. When the golden foal comes out for sale, a lot of hands go up. Mandy can barely keep up with the auctioneer. Back and forth, back and forth goes the bidding. Finally it slows, then stops. After the longest minute in Mandy's life, the auctioneer bellows "Sold!" and points to the new owner.

A Happy Ending

It's Mandy! She goes straight to the corral to welcome the new pony to the family. She's already thought of a name for the pony—Chincoteague's Sweetheart, or Sweetie for short. "The hardest part," Mandy says, "will be getting Sweetie to trust us." She's right. Sweetie will need to be "broken" before Mandy can even think of riding her. Breaking a horse means getting it used to having a bit in its mouth, a bridle on its head, and a saddle and rider on its back. It's hard work, but with love and patience, Mandy's sure to win her pony's heart.

Mini Horses

A horse the size of a dog? Is it possible? Yes! Roxanna P. can prove it. Her favorite horse, Mr. Austin, is less than three feet tall! Roxanna trains and cares for miniature horses on her grandfather's farm.

Horse Sizes

Horses are measured in *hands*, units of four inches, from the *withers*, or shoulder bones, to the ground. Miniature horses measure 34 inches or less in height. Some are as short as two feet tall! Ponies measure between 35 and 58 inches, and horses are more than 58 inches—twice the size of a mini!

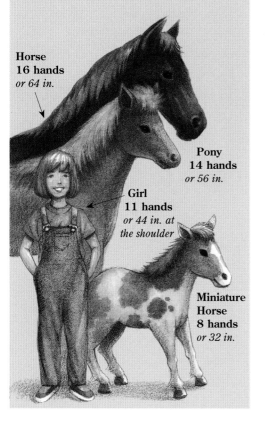

Horse
16 hands
or 64 in.

Pony
14 hands
or 56 in.

Girl
11 hands
or 44 in. at the shoulder

Miniature Horse
8 hands
or 32 in.

Pet Horses

Miniature horses are just like full-size horses but a lot easier to handle. They're perfect for kids because of their small size and friendly nature. In fact, some people treat their mini horses just like family pets, and even let them in the house! But mini horses can do a lot more than just keep you company.

Showing Off

All year long, Roxanna and Mr. Austin practice for the special mini-horse shows they compete in during the summer. The shows feature jumping and cart driving, among other events. To make sure Mr. Austin looks his best for a show, Roxanna applies special horse makeup to his eyes and hair spray to his mane and tail. She also paints his hooves black. The focus of a mini-horse show is not on the owners. It's on the animals and how graceful and well trained they are. The more blue ribbons a horse wins during the show circuit, the more valuable the horse is.

Competition Bound

Mini horses compete in several different classes at shows. Each class evaluates the horse on different skills or features.

Jumping Classes

Mini horses are too small to be ridden. So handlers lead the horses through a course of at least four jumps up to two feet high. If the horse knocks down a jump or refuses to go over, it loses points.

Hunter Classes

Hunter classes also involve jumping, but it's not how high the horse goes that matters. It's the grace and appearance the horse has as it runs through the course.

Halter Classes

These classes judge the horses by their *conformation*, or features, and how they pose. It's all about beauty!

Obstacle Classes

A horse and handler must make it through a series of obstacles, such as passing through a gate, walking over boards, and squeezing between hay bales. The class is a test of the mini horse's training and trust.

Driving Classes

Mini horses can pull carts and buggies. They perform at both a walk and a trot and are judged by how well the vehicle, horse, and driver work together.

Babysitting

Roxanna works to train Mr. Austin several afternoons a week. She also helps her grandfather care for his mini horses—more than 20 of them! One of her favorite jobs is handling the baby horses, called *foals*. Mini-horse foals are usually only about a foot and a half tall when they're born. Roxanna cuddles them like babies so that they get used to human contact. "We play with them and try to teach them not to nip or kick," Roxanna says. "But you never know what they're going to do." Mini horses are so full of personality, they're as fun to babysit as children!

Imagine being so good at gymnastics that you can do hand-
stands, back bends, and walkovers—all on the jiggling back
of a cantering horse! Julie K. does all these moves as part
of a horse-vaulting team. In vaulting, girls and boys compete
together and as individuals, doing both compulsory moves and
kürs (pronounced "cures"), or freestyle routines, to music. Their
performances are scored on a scale of one to ten, according
to how well they move and how graceful their routines are.
Instead of riding gear, vaulters wear unitards and slippers!

The Horse

The horse is a lot more than something for the vaulters to ride on—it's another member of the team. Most teams use big, gentle horse breeds, such as Belgians and Clydesdales. The horse trains for up to four years, getting used to being guided around and around the vaulting ring on the longe line, and to wearing a leather vaulting *surcingle* (SUR-sing-gull), or wide strap with padded handles, rather than a saddle. Most of all, the horse has to get used to all the jumps of the vaulters!

Practice

Julie's team practices twice a week during fall and winter. They try out new moves on a barrel first. Only when they've perfected a new routine do they try it on a moving horse. The horse canters around a ring, guided by a *longe* (lunj) line. It's very steady, but even so, it can be a bit scary. No one should try it without getting the special training it requires!

In summer, Julie's team practices every day for six hours. It's a lot of work, but the girls have to be good. They plan to compete nationally.

Compulsory Competition Moves

In competition, vaulters must perform seven compulsory moves. The first is a dramatic vault onto a horse while it canters around the ring. Then vaulters show their skill in the following six moves. All are performed in time to music that the vaulters choose.

Mill

Vaulters turn all the way around on the horse in this move, shown below. There are four basic phases. In each, one leg is raised as high as possible in front of the vaulter and passed over the horse's body. Each difficult leg position must be held for four canter strides.

Basic Riding Seat

The rider sits astride the horse, with both arms extended to the sides. The shoulders, hips, and heels all need to be in a perfect line, and the rider has to hold the position for four canter strides. If her legs are too far forward, her back is arched, or she looks too stiff, she can lose points.

Flag

This move, shown left, mimics the shape of the horse. From the basic seat, the rider grips the surcingle handles and swings up into a kneel. Then she raises her inside arm and outside leg at the same time to form a smooth arc. Shoulders and hips have to stay level.

Scissors

The vaulter swings her legs up behind her almost into a handstand position. Then she flips over, hands free for a moment, to land astride the horse facing backward. The move is then repeated in reverse.

Stand

From a kneel, the vaulter hops onto both feet, releases the surcingle grips, and rises to a standing position with both arms extended to the sides. The legs should absorb the motion of the horse, while the upper body remains still. The vaulter can't look down at all, or she'll lose points.

Flank

The flank is a dismount. The vaulter swings up toward a handstand position, then brings her legs down, forming a "pike." She brings both legs down on one side of the horse, swings forward for momentum, and then pushes back up toward a handstand. At the top, she pushes off the surcingle, trying to go as high as possible, and (hopefully) lands on her feet!

Competition

In the United States, horse vaulting is still a relatively new sport. But in other parts of the world, vaulting goes back thousands of years. In ancient Rome, soldiers on horseback practiced vaulting! Vaulting really took off about 50 years ago in Germany, which is why many of the words used to describe moves and equipment are German.

The sport sure has come a long way. There are more than 100 vaulting teams in America now and one national competition every year. Julie and her teammates wouldn't miss it for the world!

Show Jumper

It's one of the biggest thrills of all—jumping. Horse and rider are a perfect team, flying through the air together. It looks effortless. But it's not! Four times a week, 11-year-old Caitlin D. travels over an hour to a stable in order to train in show jumping, the sport of riding a horse or pony through a course filled with fences. Caitlin's good. She won a blue ribbon at her very first pony show!

Starting Off

Caitlin started off just like every young rider. The first step is to learn to keep your balance on horseback. Riders should be comfortable sitting astride a moving horse without holding on! The next step is to walk the horse or pony over a series of poles on the ground. The poles make the pony lift its feet high, and while the pony trots, the rider can practice getting into the right jumping position. Finally, horse and rider begin to jump very low fences. Then it just takes lots and lots of practice.

Jumping Stages

Takeoff

Bottoms up! The rider must get all of her weight out of the saddle at takeoff. But if she leans too far forward, she's just making it harder for her horse.

Flight

The actual jump is all about balance. Riders must sit straight, with their weight out of the saddle, looking forward. Leaning to one side, looking down, falling forward—all of these things make it difficult for the horse to maintain its balance.

Landing

Strong legs help absorb the impact of landing, which feels very bumpy at first! Riders have to stretch their arms forward as well, giving the horse as much rein as it needs.

The Real Thing

Once she learned to jump, it wasn't long before Caitlin was in competition. Caitlin competes in the pony hunters, a sport that can trace its roots back to British fox hunting. In this division, horses and riders are judged on their form and style as they jump a series of colored fences. Before it's her turn to ride, Caitlin spends a quiet moment alone with her pony. She needs to be calm and able to concentrate. She will be gauging the precise distance to each jump on the course so that she can tell her pony exactly when to take off. If she gets it right, each jump will look effortless and beautiful.

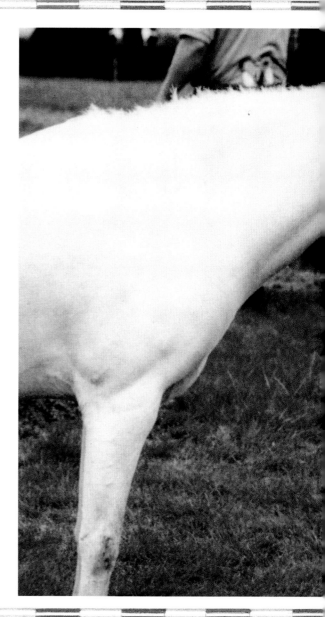

Riding Habit

To compete in a jumping show, a rider wears a special riding outfit called a *habit*.

Helmet

A hard helmet is required. It's usually covered in velvet. The helmet is sometimes called a hunt cap because it was originally worn by riders in fox hunts.

Jacket

The rider wears a close-fitting jacket made from wool, which wears well. But it can be hot in the summer sun!

Ratcatcher Shirt

In England, people used to wear casual hunting clothes to hunt rats on foot! Today, what became known as a "ratcatcher shirt" is formal enough to wear at a show. Girls often decorate their shirt collars with their initials.

Jodhpurs

Jodhpurs can be baggy around the hips or tight but stretchy so that a rider can sit comfortably on a horse.

Boots

Riders wear boots with small heels so that their feet won't slip through the stirrups.

Concentration

Caitlin memorizes the location of all the fences on the course. If she tells her pony to take off at the wrong moment, he might knock over a fence railing, or worse, refuse to jump at all!

The Payoff

Jumping is hard work, but Caitlin approaches every course with determination—and it pays off! With the help of her trainer, Caitlin hopes to win more blue ribbons in the future. But even better than blue ribbons is the time Caitlin gets to spend with her ponies. They're her partners in this sport. "Show jumping is really challenging," Caitlin says. "You have to love it!"

Rise and shine! What do you mean it's too early? There's a hungry horse waiting for you. Welcome to life on a horse farm. By 6:00 A.M. every day, Sydney H. is up and off to the stalls to feed her two ponies, Smokey Bear and Count, and to help with all the other horses. Her family raises Thoroughbreds and trains them to be racehorses, so everyone at Far Cry Farm is busy.

The Basics

Before school, Sydney carries small bales of hay, or dried grass, to the horses' stalls. A 1,000-pound horse needs 7.5 pounds of hay in the morning and another 7.5 pounds of hay at night. Next Sydney pumps water. Horses can drink anywhere from 5 to 20 gallons of water a day!

Turn Out

Then Sydney *turns out* the horses, or leads them into a field where they can eat grass all day. But it's not just any old field. Sydney and her family have to maintain their farm's pastures carefully.

Field Check
The Right Fit
The field needs to be big—at least 1.5 acres —so that horses can romp and roll and run.

Poison!
Horses can become seriously sick from eating something as innocent-looking as acorns! The field must be checked for signs of poisonous plants such as henbane, rag-wort, hemlock, ground ivy, foxglove, horse-tail, buttercup, laurel, oak, privet, yew, and laburnum.

Cool Drinks
There must be a good water source in the field.

Tree House
Trees provide horses with shelter from wind and rain. If the field is treeless, there should be some kind of shelter.

Fencing
Horses do wander. The fence around the field must be in good condition.

Two's Company
Horses like company and usually should have a field mate.

Mucking Out
Dig In
First Sydney uses a pitchfork and shovel to scoop out all the piles of droppings in the stalls and to dump them in a bucket. Any wet or really dirty bedding is forked into the bucket, too.

Clean Sweep
The floor and corners must be swept clean. Then the bucket is dumped in a manure pile. The pile should be far away! Manure attracts flies, and flies bother horses.

All Set
Fresh bedding should be forked all around the edges of the stalls. Bedding is deep enough when the tines of the pitchfork won't reach the floor when the fork is held upright.

Clean Up
The horses are free to frolic in the field, but Sydney heads back to the stables to *muck out*, or clean, their stalls. She removes the soiled bedding, which is full of manure, and replaces it with fresh bedding. Mucking out takes about half an hour. Then Sydney moves fast. She needs a shower before school!

Playtime

When Sydney gets home from school, the horses are waiting for her. But now it's time for fun! She checks her ponies over and removes any clumps of dirt before she *tacks up,* or puts a saddle and bridle on a pony for a ride. Each pony needs to be exercised for at least 20 minutes. Sometimes just tacking up can be a workout!

Bridle

Saddle

Tack

Sydney uses English-style tack, which is stream-lined so that the rider can always be in very close contact with the horse.

Bridle

The bridle goes over the pony's head. The nose-band and browband hold it in place.

Bit

The bit goes in the pony's mouth and is attached to the reins. When the rider pulls on the reins, the pony feels it in its mouth and slows down or stops.

Saddle

The saddle sits on a saddle blanket to protect the pony's back and keep the saddle clean.

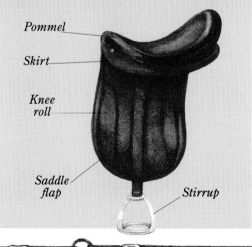

Pommel

Skirt

Knee roll

Saddle flap

Stirrup

Headstall

Browband

Noseband

Reins

Bit

Grooming

After exercising the ponies, Sydney has to groom them. She *curries,* or cleans, them with a currycomb to loosen dirt, dead hair, and tangles. She uses a brush to make their coats lie flat, and a comb to make their manes and tails smooth. She also uses a hoof pick to clean out any mud and manure in their hooves.

A Final Scrub

Every time she rides, Sydney has to clean her tack, too. Clean tack is more comfortable for her ponies, and it will last a lot longer for her. She rubs everything down with *saddle soap,* a thick, pastelike wax that removes dirt and keeps leather soft and shiny. The bit needs to be cleaned, too. Sydney puts it in the dishwasher!

Saddle soap

Currycomb

Body brush

Hoof pick

Comb

A Hard Day's Work

Finally Sydney stocks up the ponies' stalls for the night. She lugs in more water buckets and gets several more pounds of hay. By the time the ponies are settled, she's more than ready for bed. She hardly has a moment to herself, but she wouldn't trade her lifestyle for the world. The love Smokey Bear and Count show her and the good times she shares with them make all the hard work worthwhile.

If you want to be around horses, you need to learn some basics, like how a horse's body is put together, how to describe a horse's colors and markings, and how to understand a horse's feelings. Read on to gather some horse sense!

Poll

Crest

Croup

Loins

Withers

Muzzle

Dock

Shoulder

Chest

Pony Points

The parts of a horse or pony are called its points. You'll want to know your horse's basic points in order to keep your horse healthy.

Gaskin

Elbow

Forearm

Cannon

Fetlock

Pastern

Knee

Hock

Coronet

Hoof

Colors

Horses come in many colors because in the wild their color helped to *camouflage*, or hide, them from predators. There is an astonishing variety of shades and colors. These are the basic color ranges.

Appaloosa

Blue Roan

Strawberry Roan

White

Black

Brown

Gray

Palomino

Markings

Horses have unique leg and facial markings. These are the most common.

Blaze

Snip

Star

Stripe

Coronet

Sock

Stocking

Dun

Chestnut

Bay

Communication

Relax!

A content, relaxed horse will often rest the toe of a back leg on the ground. Its ears will be up and turned slightly aside.

On the Alert

Ears pricked forward mean a horse is very interested in something. You'll probably see this expression at mealtime!

Grrrrr!

A horse will lift a back leg to show that it is about to kick if it doesn't like something. Its ears will turn back, its nostrils will flare, and it may even show its teeth.

Flat Ears

If a horse's ears are laid back flat, it is scared, confused, or angry.

Rabbit Ears

Watch carefully. You'll see when your horse is listening. His ears will be turning every which way!

Heavy Breathing

Horses whinny to one another; nicker a friendly greeting; snort when anxious; blow, sigh, grunt, groan, and even scream when in pain.

Horse Sense

Important Note

American Girl offers these Web site addresses as a source of information for you and your parents. We can't guarantee that the sites listed will give you the exact information you need, or that the addresses won't change after this book is printed. Always share information you get online with your parents, and never give out personal information.

Web Sites

www.assateague.com has information about the wild horses on Assateague Island.

www.cowgirls.com has lots of rodeo fun for cowgirls of all ages.

www.americanvaulting.org has great pictures of vaulting competitions.

www.amha.com has miniature-horse history and current news.

www.usef.org has news about nearly every equestrian sport.

www.horseadvice.com has advice on horse care.

Pony Club

Pony Club, a special group for horse and pony lovers like you, will teach you all about riding and grooming, caring for horses and ponies, and riding safely. Best of all, you don't even need your own horse! You can arrange to borrow one for riding practice through the club. Over 400 Pony Clubs exist in the U.S.— and there are more Pony Clubs all over the world! To find out more, check out the Pony Club Web site at **www.ponyclub.org** or call (859)254-PONY.

4-H

Local branches of the 4-H Club also offer horse programs for kids ages 7 to 19. The programs offer different kinds of care and riding instructions, such as for English or Western riding, depending on where you live. For more information, contact your local 4-H Club. A full listing of 4-H Clubs can be found at **www.national4-hheadquarters.gov/about/4h_map.htm**.

Saddle up!